In the Footsteps of Explorers

Sieur de La Salle
New World Adventurer

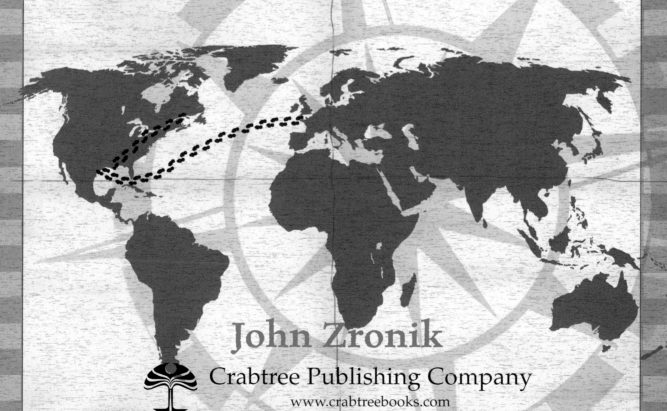

John Zronik

Crabtree Publishing Company
www.crabtreebooks.com

Crabtree Publishing Company

www.crabtreebooks.com

To J.O.

Coordinating editor: Ellen Rodger
Series editor: Carrie Gleason
Project editor: Rachel Eagen
Editor: Adrianna Morganelli
Design and production coordinator: Rosie Gowsell
Cover design and production assistance: Samara Parent
Art direction: Rob MacGregor
Scanning technician: Arlene Arch-Wilson
Photo research: Allison Napier

Consultants: Stacy Hasselbacher and Tracey L. Neikirk, Museum Educators, The Mariners' Museum

Photo Credits: AP/ Wide World Photos: p. 20, p. 27 (top); The Art Archive/ Musée des Arts Africans et Océaniens/ Dagli Orti: cover; Werner Forman/ Art Resource, NY: p. 24 (bottom); Bibliotheque Nationale, Paris, France, Giraudon/ Bridgeman Art Library: p. 12; Bibliotheque Nationale, Paris, France, Lauros, Giraudon/ Bridgeman Art Library: p. 25; Library of Congress, Washington D.C, USA/ Bridgeman Art Library: p. 11; Private Collection;/ Bridgeman Art Library: p. 14, p. 19 (top); Bettmann/ Corbis: p. 23 (top); Gunter Marx Photography/ Corbis: p. 29; Nathan Benn/ Corbis: 22; The Granger Collection: p. 5, p. 7, p. 28; iStock Photo: p. 15; North Wind Picture Archives: p. 8 (top), p. 13, p. 17, p. 21, p. 24 (top), pp. 26-27; Other images from stock photo cd

Illustrations: Lauren Fast: p. 6 (top); Dennis Gregory Teakle: p. 4; David Wysotski, Allure Illustrations: pp. 18-19

Cartography: Jim Chernishenko: title page, p. 10

Cover: La Salle built several forts and trading posts during his voyages through the American wilderness.

Title page: La Salle traveled the length of the Mississippi River and claimed a large region of the United States for France. He named the region Louisiana, for King Louis XIV.

Sidebar icon: La Salle and his crew came across many different animals as they traveled through the American wilderness, such as bears, foxes, and the bald eagle, which is now the national bird of the United States.

Crabtree Publishing Company

www.crabtreebooks.com   1-800-387-7650

Cataloging-in-Publication Data
Zronik, John Paul, 1972-
   Sieur de La Salle: New World adventurer / written by John Zronik.
      p. cm. -- (In the footsteps of explorers)
   Includes index.
   ISBN-13: 978-0-7787-2413-1 (rlb)
   ISBN-10: 0-7787-2413-1 (rlb)
   ISBN-13: 978-0-7787-2449-0 (pbk)
   ISBN-10: 0-7787-2449-2 (pbk)
1. La Salle, Robert Cavelier, Sieur de, 1643-1687--Juvenile literature. 2. Explorers--North America--Biography--Juvenile literature. 3. Explorers--France--Biography--Juvenile literature. 4. Canada--Discovery and exploration--French--Juvenile literature. 5. Canada--History--To 1763 (New France)--Juvenile literature. 6. Mississippi River Valley--Discovery and exploration--French--Juvenile literature. I. Title. II. Series.
   F1030.5.Z76 2005
   910'.92--dc22   2005014835
                                                                    LC

**Published in
the United States**
PMB 16A
350 Fifth Ave.
Suite 3308
New York, NY
10118

**Published
in Canada**
616 Welland Ave.
St. Catharines
Ontario, Canada
L2M 5V6

**Published in the
United Kingdom**
73 Lime Walk
Headington
Oxford
OX3 7AD
United Kingdom

**Published
in Australia**
386 Mt. Alexander Rd.
Ascot Vale (Melbourne)
V1C 3032

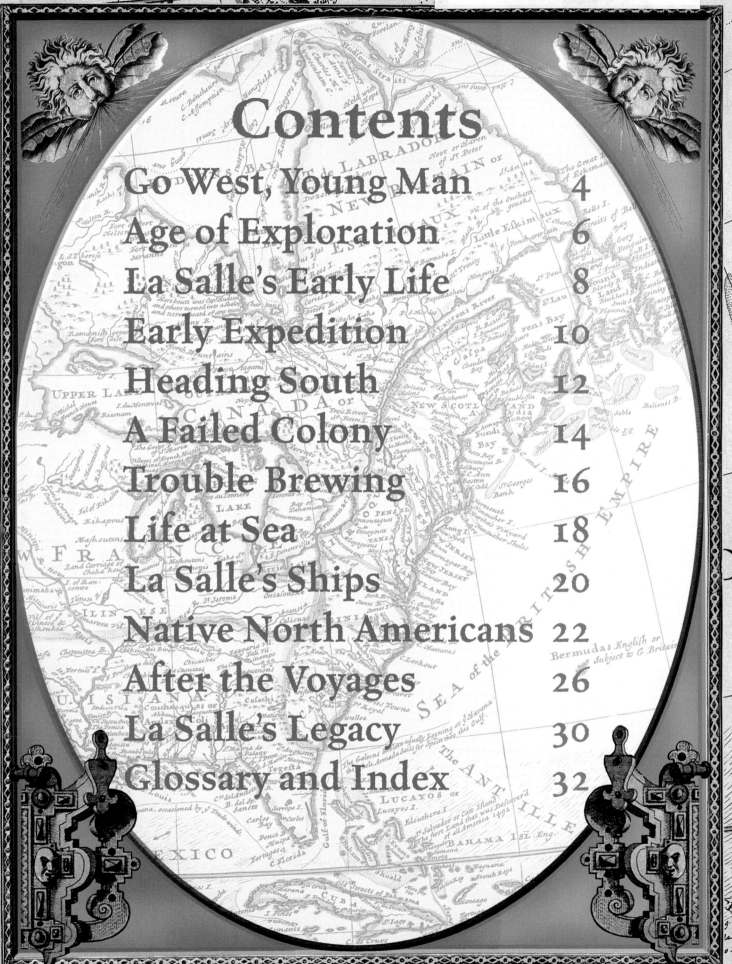

Contents

Go West, Young Man

René Robert Cavelier, Sieur de La Salle, was one of the great explorers of the New World. Born and raised in France, La Salle became famous for his exploration of many lakes and rivers in North America.

Exploring North America

La Salle was the first European to travel the entire length of the Mississippi River to the Gulf of Mexico, where he hoped to establish a French colony. La Salle's travels covered a large area of North America. He spent some time navigating the Great Lakes region before exploring the area now known as the southern United States. La Salle explored under the authority of King Louis XIV of France. La Salle is most famous for claiming the lands around the Mississippi River Valley. He named these lands Louisiana after his king.

What's in a Name?

During the 1600s in France, a young man born into a wealthy family was usually called by the name of his family's estate and was addressed as "sieur," the French word for "sir." La Salle was the name of the Cavelier family estate, so René Robert Cavelier eventually became known as "Sieur de La Salle," or Sir of La Salle.

(above) La Salle helped France become more powerful by building trading posts and claiming lands in North America.

In a Strange Land

Explorers in the New World met up with people who did not speak the same language, and misunderstandings sometimes ended in bloodshed. La Salle did not keep journals of his travels, but two other explorers, Jolliet and Marquette, traveled in the same region as La Salle, and reported their adventures in letters to their superiors. In the following letter, Marquette writes of an encounter with a group of Native North American warriors near the Arkansas River. No one was hurt during this confrontation.

"They were armed with bows, arrows, hatchets, clubs and shields. They prepared to attack us, on both land and water. Some of them embarked in great wooden canoes... in order to intercept and surround us on all sides... One of them hurled his club, which passed over us without striking us... I made signs that we were not coming to war against them. The alarm continued, and they were already preparing to pierce us with arrows from all sides." -Jacques Marquette

(below) La Salle and his crew feasting with Native North Americans.

-1643-

La Salle is born on November 22 in Rouen, France.

-1667-

La Salle leaves school and arrives in the New World.

-1682-

La Salle travels the Mississippi River to the Gulf of Mexico.

-1687-

La Salle is murdered by members of his own crew.

-1492-

Christopher Columbus sails across the Atlantic Ocean, and discovers the New World.

-1498-

Vasco da Gama becomes the first European to sail from Europe to India.

-1609-

Henry Hudson (above) explores the east coast of North America.

Age of Exploration

Europeans had been exploring and settling in the New World since around 1500. They came seeking trade goods, such as furs, as well as rich soil for growing food. The French, English, and Spanish all came to North America to build colonies.

New World Settlements

By the time La Salle arrived in the New World in 1667, Spain had established colonies in South and Central America. The English and French had explored and built settlements further north, on the Atlantic Coast of North America. English and Dutch settlers built colonies in the area that is now the northeastern United States. La Salle and other French settlers built colonies further north, in present-day Quebec, Canada.

Hostile Relations

Since the 1500s, European explorers and colonists frequently had hostile relationships with the peoples who had been living in North America before the Europeans arrived. Peoples belonging to the Algonquian and Iroquoian language groups were often pushed off their lands or killed. French settlements and Native North American villages sometimes existed side by side.

Political Alliance

Over time, the French learned to build **alliances** with the Native North Americans, who could help the French find their way through the North American wilderness. They were also valuable trade partners, exchanging pelts of beaver, otter, and deer for European goods, such as guns. An alliance between the French and the Huron and Algonquian **tribes** helped the French keep their English **rivals** at bay.

French versus English

In 1609, Samuel de Champlain, the founder of a French colony called New France, ordered his troops to help the Huron and Algonquian peoples in a war against the Iroquois, or Haudenosaunee peoples. When La Salle arrived in New France, some Iroquois had signed a peace treaty with the French to end their conflict. The English eventually allied with the Iroquois. The English and French competed for lands in the West.

(background) French explorers, including La Salle, brought Christian missionaries with them on their voyages. Christianity is a religion that follows the teachings of Jesus Christ, who Christians believe is God's son. Religious leaders, called priests, preached to the Native North Americans to convert them to Christianity.

La Salle's Early Life

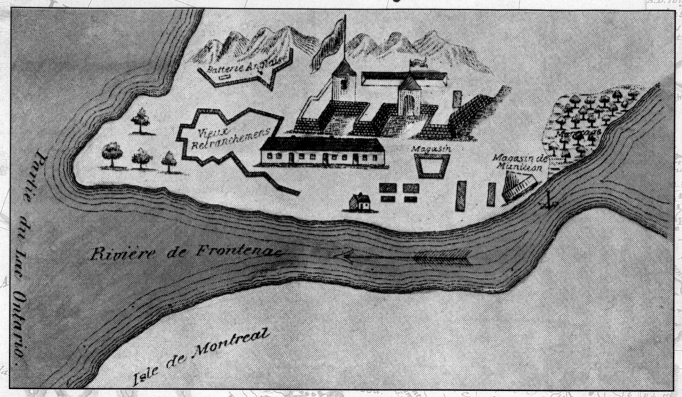

As a teenager, La Salle studied at a seminary to become a Catholic priest. He did well in his studies, but he often lost interest in his work. At the age of 22, La Salle begged his teachers to send him to China as a missionary, but they felt he was not ready because he had not completed his schooling.

A New World

On March 28, 1667, La Salle left the seminary, claiming his **morals** were too weak for the strict life of the priesthood. He decided to travel to New France, a French colony in present-day Quebec, Canada. La Salle's brother, Jean, worked as a **Sulpician** priest in New France. The Sulpicians were the "seigneurs" of Montreal, meaning they controlled the distribution of land. Seigneurs gave areas of land to other colonists for them to farm. At the time, about 10,000 colonists lived in New France, including farmers, fur traders, missionaries, and explorers. The seigneurs became very wealthy by farming food crops and trading furs, which they sent back to Europe and sold.

(top) Fort Frontenac was built in present-day Kingston, Canada.

(above) The French traded for beaver furs, which were made into hats and sold to wealthy Europeans.

La Salle's Estate

Once La Salle arrived in New France, he was granted land, or a "seigniory." As a seigneur, La Salle was a land-holding noble. He assigned plots of his land to French peasants, or habitants. The habitants paid La Salle for use of his land. La Salle also founded a village, Côte de Saint Sulpice, where he became rich by farming and trading with the local Algonquian-speaking peoples.

"La Chine"

Over time, La Salle was told of the Ohio River from the local Seneca tribe, who said that it led to a sea. La Salle hoped that the river joined the Pacific Ocean, which would give him access to the trade goods of China, such as silk and spices. He became so obsessed with the idea that his seigniory was soon nicknamed "La Chine," or China, by other settlers in New France.

(above) Spices from Asia were highly valued by Europeans.

The Northwest Passage

Despite the opportunities for wealth in the New World, many explorers set their sights on more distant lands. China was a land rich with silk, spices, and other valuable trade goods. By the late 1500s, explorers were trying to find a shortcut to China through North America. This route, called the Northwest Passage, was thought to connect the Atlantic and Pacific oceans. If found, the Northwest Passage would allow merchants to access Chinese trade goods, which could be sold to wealthy Europeans.

Early Expedition

La Salle sold his Montreal seigniory to finance an expedition across the Great Lakes. He was determined to find the Ohio River that the Seneca had told him about. His earnings from trading furs at Saint Sulpice also helped him pay for the trip.

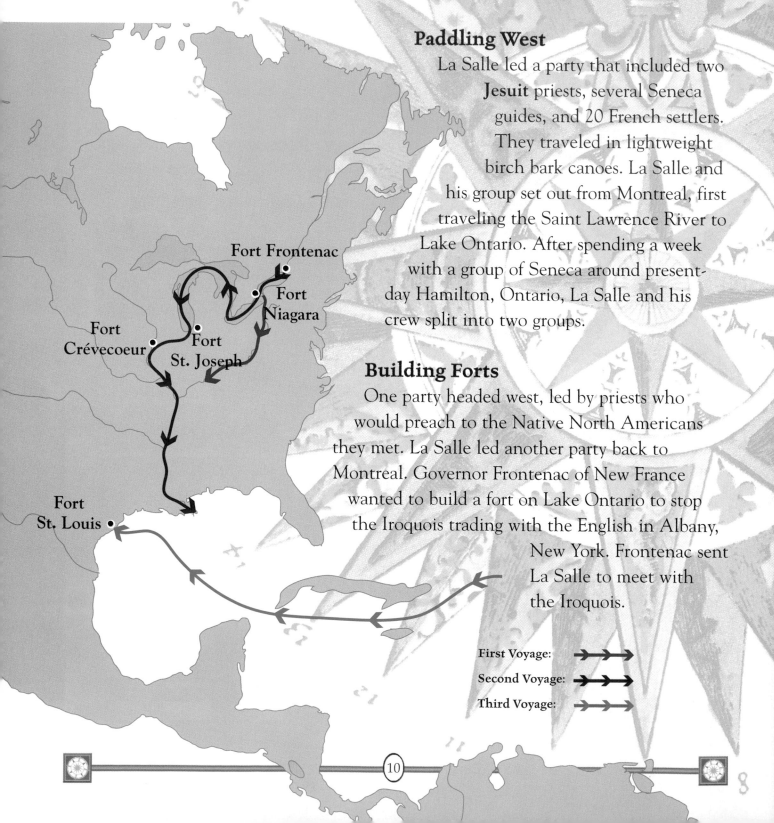

Paddling West

La Salle led a party that included two **Jesuit** priests, several Seneca guides, and 20 French settlers. They traveled in lightweight birch bark canoes. La Salle and his group set out from Montreal, first traveling the Saint Lawrence River to Lake Ontario. After spending a week with a group of Seneca around present-day Hamilton, Ontario, La Salle and his crew split into two groups.

Building Forts

One party headed west, led by priests who would preach to the Native North Americans they met. La Salle led another party back to Montreal. Governor Frontenac of New France wanted to build a fort on Lake Ontario to stop the Iroquois trading with the English in Albany, New York. Frontenac sent La Salle to meet with the Iroquois.

First Voyage:
Second Voyage:
Third Voyage:

An Agreement

The Iroquois formed a trading alliance with the French, and they also allowed the French to build a fort on the west bank of the Cataraqui River, in present-day Kingston, Ontario. La Salle was in charge of building the new fort, which later became the busy trading post called Fort Frontenac. King Louis XIV gave ownership of Fort Frontenac to La Salle, and urged him to set up new colonies in North America.

(right) La Salle's crew had never seen raccoons before they came to North America.

(below) The French obtained permission from the Iroquois to build a fort on their land.

-1669-

La Salle sells his seigniory in New France and makes his first journey through North America.

-1672-

Louis de Baude Frontenac becomes governor of New France.

-1673-

La Salle builds Fort Frontenac.

-1682-

La Salle claims Louisiana for France.

A Failed Colony

La Salle discovered a powerful enemy soon after his voyage to the Gulf of Mexico. In 1682, Governor Frontenac was replaced by Joseph-Antoine La Barre. La Barre disapproved of La Salle's voyages, and he removed Fort Frontenac from La Salle's control.

New Goals

La Salle knew by this point the rivers he had been traveling did not lead to China. His dream of finding the Northwest Passage was replaced by another goal. La Salle dreamed of building a large trading post at the mouth of the Mississippi, where it empties into the Gulf of Mexico. European ships traveling along the Atlantic coast would give La Salle a lot of business and make him a very rich man. Governor La Barre did not support La Salle and would not **fund** his voyage. La Salle went to France to talk with King Louis XIV.

(background) King Louis XIV first thought that La Salle's voyages were worthless, but changed his mind when La Salle claimed that they could overtake Spanish territory along the Mississippi.

Lying to the King

Knowing King Louis wanted to take over Spanish territory, which lay to the west of Louisiana, La Salle made up a lie to get the king to support him. He told the king that the Mississippi River was close to the Rio Grande in New Spain. He **tampered** with maps and claimed that the Mississippi was 746 miles (1,200 kilometers) further west than it really was. La Salle said that the Mississippi was an ideal place for launching an attack.

Royal Backing

La Salle's lies worked, and King Louis gave him permission to build a French colony where the Mississippi River meets the Gulf of Mexico. La Salle loaded five ships with 300 settlers, including soldiers, **carpenters**, and farmers. As they set sail for the New World, the settlers did not know that La Salle had not drawn maps of the region during his previous voyage. He did not know how to reach the Mississippi from the Gulf of Mexico.

(below) La Salle told King Louis that the Rio Grande River was close to the Mississippi. The Rio Grande ran through Spanish territory.

-1684-

La Salle's
final
expedition
departs for
the Gulf
of Mexico.

-1685-

La Salle's
party arrives
at Matagorda
Bay, Texas.

-1686-

The *Belle*
sinks at
Matagorda
Bay.

-1687-

La Salle is
shot
and killed.

Trouble Brewing

One of La Salle's ships was captured by Spanish pirates on the Atlantic. The *Saint Francis* had been carrying building supplies and food for the settlers. The loss of the ship was only the first serious problem for La Salle on what would become a disastrous journey.

Disaster Strikes

La Salle's sense of direction failed him once he entered the Gulf of Mexico. He sailed 500 miles (805 kilometers) past the Mississippi delta, landing at Matagorda Bay, Texas. Soon after landing, his ship, the *Aimable*, ran **aground** in the shallow waters of the bay. Some of the settlers returned to France onboard another ship, the *Joly*. Many settlers died from **malnutrition** while trying to build a permanent settlement.

Stranded

The situation worsened when the *Belle*, La Salle's last remaining ship, sank in Matagorda Bay. The colonists were stranded. La Salle led small parties on foot to try to locate the Mississippi River. He hoped to get supplies at Fort St. Louis, a fort that he had built with Henri de Tonti at Starved Rock, Illinois, the previous year. He would then bring his crew and the colonists up to New France. The long journey back north was La Salle's best chance for the survival of his crew and the colonists.

A Discontented Crew

La Salle's attempts to find the Mississippi weakened his crew. His men were dying off every day from disease and in attacks from a group of local peoples known as the Karankawa. The remaining crew desperately wanted to go home, but La Salle demanded they travel on foot through the wilderness to find the rivers that would lead them back to New France.

The Death of La Salle

After being stranded in the wilderness for two years, La Salle's crew reached their breaking point. During a **trek** to find the Mississippi, a few of La Salle's men walked ahead of the group and hid in the tall grass. As La Salle approached, one of the men, Pierre Duhaut, shot La Salle in the face. He fell dead on the spot.

(background) After the crew murdered La Salle, they stripped him of his clothing and took his belongings. La Salle's obsession with building a colony at the mouth of the Mississippi caused him to lose the respect of his crew because he refused to give up on his mission, even though it meant the death of most of his crew and fellow colonists.

Life at Sea

La Salle and his crew faced many hardships during their cross-Atlantic voyages. Faring the high seas meant facing rough weather, illnesses, food shortages, and pirates.

Daily Life

Crew members shared cramped, dirty quarters at sea. Everyone slept below the main deck, in **hammocks** that they hung from wall to wall. Only the captain had his own room and a proper bed. Bathing was impossible, and most of the crew were plagued by lice and fleas that lived in the sailors' hair.

(below) Barrels were used for storing fresh drinking water and an alcoholic drink called ale. Most foods rotted in the humid sea air, so meat had to be preserved with plenty of salt. Dried meat and peas, as well as fish caught on the voyage, were common ship fare.

Pemmican

Pemmican is a traditional Native North American food made from dried meat. Pemmican was taken on long journeys or hunting trips into the wilderness because it did not spoil for long periods of time.

Ingredients:
2 ounces (57 grams) beef jerky
4 dried apple slices
A handful of raisins, dried cranberries, or dried cherries

Directions:
1. Place beef jerky in a food processor and grind until finely chopped.
2. Add the dried fruit. Grind until finely chopped.
3. Empty the mixture onto a sheet of wax paper. Lay another sheet of wax paper on top.
4. Use a rolling pin to flatten the pemmican until it is about 1/8 inch (3 millimeters) thick.
5. Let the pemmican dry for two days in the sun, or bake it in an oven at 350°F (175°C) for two hours. Turn it several times as it dries.
7. Once dry, break the pemmican into several pieces to eat as a snack.

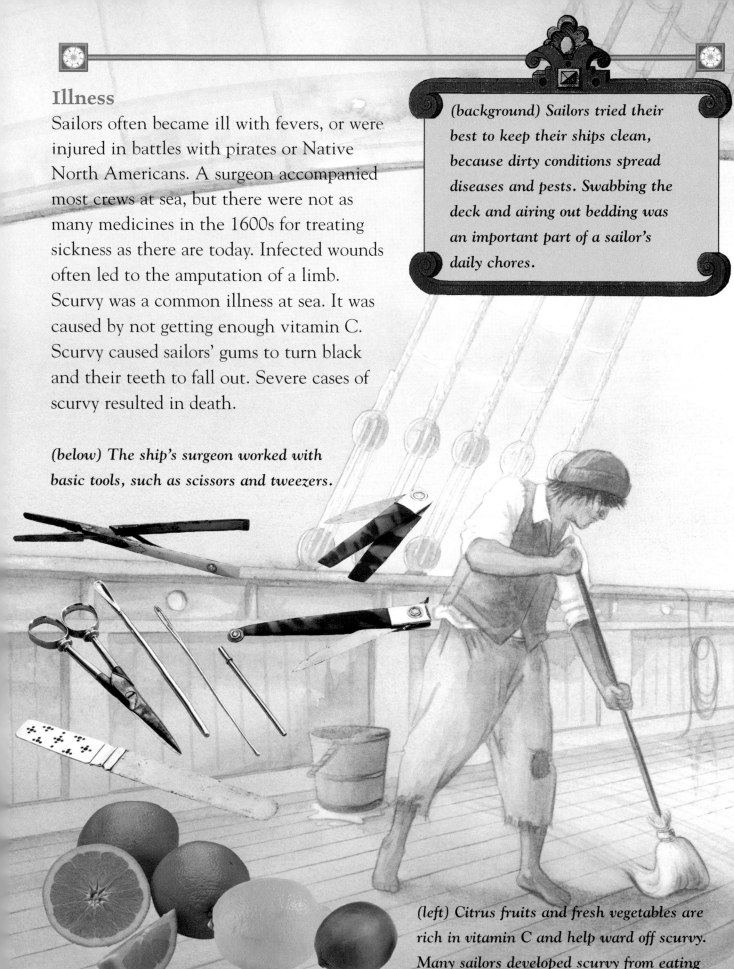

Illness

Sailors often became ill with fevers, or were injured in battles with pirates or Native North Americans. A surgeon accompanied most crews at sea, but there were not as many medicines in the 1600s for treating sickness as there are today. Infected wounds often led to the amputation of a limb. Scurvy was a common illness at sea. It was caused by not getting enough vitamin C. Scurvy caused sailors' gums to turn black and their teeth to fall out. Severe cases of scurvy resulted in death.

(below) The ship's surgeon worked with basic tools, such as scissors and tweezers.

(background) Sailors tried their best to keep their ships clean, because dirty conditions spread diseases and pests. Swabbing the deck and airing out bedding was an important part of a sailor's daily chores.

(left) Citrus fruits and fresh vegetables are rich in vitamin C and help ward off scurvy. Many sailors developed scurvy from eating mostly meat and hard biscuits at sea.

La Salle's Ships

The four ships La Salle brought across the ocean were different sizes and used for different purposes. Larger warships, such as the *Joly*, were used for carrying supplies. Smaller vessels, called canoes, were used on the narrow rivers of North America.

Ocean Vessels

Ships for sea travel were large, heavy boats made of strong timber. The ships had tall sides that could withstand the constant thrashing of large ocean waves. Large sails were rectangular or **lateen** in shape, and were attached to large posts called masts. Sailors guided the sails using long ropes to catch the wind and propel the ship forward. Supplies, such as ropes, food, and trade goods, were kept beneath the deck.

Canoes

La Salle and his crew navigated the narrow rivers of North America by canoe. Native North Americans had been traveling this way for hundreds of years. They crafted their canoes by stretching birch bark over wooden frames. The boats were light enough to carry over land, and large enough to accommodate several passengers and supplies. Canoes were also ideal for traveling in shallow water.

Discovering the *Belle*

The *Belle* remained buried in mud for over 300 years after it sank. Archaeologist J. Barto Arnold and his team began the long process of excavating and preserving the ship in 1995. The team has brought up a large piece of the *Belle*'s hull, as well as many other items, such as guns, dishes, and a large bronze cannon weighing about 800 pounds (363 kilograms).

(right) A skeleton was found among the wreckage of the Belle.

(background) Some historians believe La Salle thought he had found a branch of the Mississippi when he landed at Matagorda Bay, Texas.

Native North Americans

There were many tribes of Native North Americans living in the area east of the Mississippi River during the 1600s. Most of them belonged to one of two different language groups, Algonquian, or Iroquoian. Some of them shared similar traditions.

Hunting

The Native North Americans that La Salle and his crew encountered lived in groups of related families, or tribes. They relied on their natural environment for survival. They used a bow and arrow to hunt deer, rabbit, bear, buffalo, and beaver. They also fished in lakes, rivers, and streams, catching different types of water fowl, fish, and even turtles.

Homes

Some of the Algonquian and Iroquoian-speaking peoples that La Salle met made homes by bending young tree saplings into a frame, which they covered with tree bark, animal skins, or woven mats. The Powhatan, an Algonquian group that lived in present-day Virginia, called their homes *yehakins*. In the north, Algonquian and Iroquoian speakers made smaller homes known as wigwams.

(above) The Iroquois who lived in what is now Ontario, Canada, and New York State, built longhouses. In winter, the doors at either end of the houses were covered with animal skins to keep out the wind.

(left) Tree sap was boiled over a fire to make syrup.

(bottom) Some Native North Americans traveled in canoes they made from birch bark. Others made canoes from hollowed-out trees.

Farming and Gathering

Men cleared the fields and women helped plant them. Tribes in all parts of North America hunted, gathered and fished for food. Some farmed crops such as corn, pumpkin, beets, and squash. They also ate wild foods from the forest, such as berries, apples, and nuts. The Miami tribe, an Algonquian group, tapped maple trees to get their sap, which was used to make maple syrup.

Trade

When Europeans arrived, Native North Americans began trading animal furs for European goods, such as metal tools and guns. The French could easily trade a small amount of alcohol and receive eight times the amount in furs from different Native North American groups. Furs were extremely valuable in Europe at this time. Pelts were used to make expensive hats and clothing.

Spirituality

Some Native North Americans believed in a "great spirit" that gave life to all things. Animals and plants found in nature were important spiritual symbols for tribes of both the Algonquian and Iroquoian language groups. Spiritual leaders were called shamans, or medicine men. They helped heal the sick and injured with natural **remedies** and by sending prayers to the spirit world. Shamans made medicines from plants found in the forests.

(above) The Iroquois peoples wore masks in ceremonies to communicate with the spirit world. They believed that angry spirits caused harm to people, such as illnesses and crop failure. Ceremonies were held to make the spirits happy.

(background) Shamans chanted to the spirits, prepared medicines from plants, and told stories to help heal the sick.

Relations with the Europeans

In the years leading up to La Salle's travels, the French had extended their chain of trading posts south and west in North America with the help of their Native allies. Many had become used to the French living on their land.

Many Native peoples wanted the Europeans to respect their territories. La Salle traveled with Native North American **guides**, who knew the wilderness. Without Native guides, explorers could not navigate major rivers.

(left) Native North Americans did not always accept Europeans living on their territory, or allow themselves to be converted to Christianity. This illustration shows Native North Americans killing Jesuit missionaries.

Karankawa

The Karankawa were a group of semi-nomadic Native North Americans who lived along the Gulf Coast of present-day Texas. It is believed that they migrated between the mainland and small islands along the coast, depending on the climate and the availability of food. The Karankawa first encountered Europeans nearly a century before La Salle's ships arrived. Spanish colonists had lived in Karankawa territory for almost six years. After La Salle and his crew landed at Matagorda Bay, fights between La Salle's men and the Karankawa resulted in many deaths. The Karankawa no longer exist as a group today.

After the Voyages

New France began as a small colony, but La Salle's expeditions helped expand French power in North America. La Salle built forts that gave the French access to the fur trade. Claiming the large territory of Louisiana also helped establish France in the New World.

-1680-

Fort Crévecoeur is destroyed. An Iroquois settlement is built in its place.

-1722-

Spanish soldiers build a settlement on top of the ruins of Fort St. Louis.

-1758-

Fort Frontenac is captured by British troops.

Expedition Survivors

Some of the men on La Salle's final expedition fled after the murder of La Salle. They were captured by the Spanish on the Gulf of Mexico. Some believe that other crew members lived with local groups of Native North Americans. Henri de Tonti went back to Fort St. Louis, where he was a successful seigneur, or landowner, for a short period of time. The fort was eventually abandoned in ruins. Native North Americans may have destroyed the fort in an attack against the French.

(background) La Salle's exploration of the Mississippi River to the Gulf of Mexico allowed the French to establish settlements that helped keep English expansion at bay. La Salle's routes through the United States provided new opportunities for trade.

(above) *French cannons uncovered from Fort St. Louis, built in 1683.*

Building Forts

La Salle established several forts throughout Canada and the United States. The forts were protected camps where the settlers lived while they traded, explored local lands and waterways, or built boats for further travel. The forts took several months to build. Walls made of wooden posts surrounded the grounds to protect against outside attack.

What Happened to the Forts?

Fort Frontenac was eventually captured by the English in the 1700s. Fort Crévecoeur was abandoned after a rebellion by La Salle's crew. Later, a new settlement was built over the site by the Iroquois. Fort St. Louis was a temporary settlement that was built when La Salle's crew was abandoned at Matagorda Bay. The fort did not last, as the settlers died from malnutrition, and in attacks by the local Karankawa. Spanish soldiers eventually built over the remains of Fort St. Louis.

Changing Lives

The arrival of Europeans forever changed the lives of the Native North Americans. Explorers to the New World brought trade items such as finely woven European clothing, iron pots, guns, and other metal tools. These items changed the way Native North Americans lived. While some European trade goods made life easier, the introduction of European customs meant many Native traditions were lost.

(right) Built under the Chicago River in 1871, the La Salle Tunnel, named for the explorer, reduced traffic jams until it closed in 1939.

The Louisiana Purchase

The large Louisiana territory claimed by La Salle in 1682 stretched from the mouth of the Mississippi River at the Gulf of Mexico, all the way to the Rocky Mountains in the north. The territory was purchased from France by Spain in 1762. Many nations wanted control of the region, because it was in the heart of rich fur trading grounds. France regained ownership of Louisiana in 1800 under the Treaty of Ildefonso. Then, in 1803, the United States, a small nation at the time, bought Louisiana from France for $15 million. The Louisiana Purchase doubled the size of the United States. The purchase included the vast Mississippi River and its surrounding lands.

Reservations are protected Native North American lands. In Canada, they are called reserves.

The Cost

The Europeans brought diseases with them, including fevers that killed many Native North Americans, who did not have **immunity** against them. Native North Americans also lost an enormous amount of their territory as Europeans settlements moved further inland. Christian missionaries discouraged Native North American beliefs in the spirits that they had depended on for protection. Religious ceremonies devoted to these spirits were prevented or even **outlawed**.

(below) Deer pelts were used to make clothing. Unlike some animals that were hunted for the fur trade, North American deer remain plentiful.

Living Traditions

Today, Native North Americans continue to keep their rich culture alive through their artwork and spiritual beliefs. Powwows, or social gatherings, are still held in Native North American communities. Powwows feature traditional drumming, singing, and dancing.

La Salle's Legacy

In some parts of North America, La Salle's name remains a part of people's everyday lives. Many places were named after La Salle, including La Salle County, Illinois, and the city of La Salle, Quebec. Museums house artifacts from Fort St. Louis, and from the sunken ship, the *Belle*.

Lasting Influence

Even though La Salle did not succeed in building a large trading post at the mouth of the Mississippi, La Salle did help establish French power in the New World. His establishment of forts, and his navigation of the Mississippi River paved the way for further European settlement in the West.

The Fur Trade

In the years following La Salle's expeditions, the fur trade took a serious toll on animal populations. Once-abundant species, such as beaver and mink, became more difficult to find, and in some areas, were driven to **extinction**. Despite the fur trade's impact, the animals sought after by Europeans at the time of La Salle are still common in parts of North America today. Conservation programs are in place to preserve these animals.

Named After La Salle

Several small towns in North America are named after the explorer who helped map them, such as La Salle Parish in the state of Louisiana. La Salle is also a town on the banks of the Detroit River in Canada. It began as a small community built by French settlers, but is now a popular port town. The car company General Motors named a car after the man who explored so much of North America. The La Salle car was manufactured from 1927 to 1940.

The City of La Salle

The city of La Salle stands in the place of La Salle's first fort, Saint Sulpice. La Salle is located on the south shore of Montreal Island in present-day Quebec, Canada. The local Lachine Rapids are a constant reminder of La Salle's dream of finding a passage to China, as well as Saint Sulpice's nickname, "La Chine."

(background) The Ohio River runs through present-day Louisville, Kentucky. La Salle traveled the Ohio during his first voyage into what is now known as the southern United States.

Glossary

aground To scrape along the bottom of an ocean or river

alliance A group of people who help each other

carpenter A woodworker

colony Territory that is ruled by another country

convert To change into something else, usually into a follower of another religion

estate Property owned by one person or a family

excavate To dig up

extinct The state of being completely wiped out, such as a species of animals that no longer exists

fund To give someone money to do something

guide A person who leads another person or group of people through unknown land

hammock A bed that is suspended between two points

immunity The body's defense against diseases

Jesuits An organization of Catholic priests who preached Christianity in the New World

lateen Triangular in shape

malnutrition Sickness that results from not eating enough foods that are rich in vitamins for staying healthy

missionary Someone who goes to another country to preach to a group of people in an attempt to get them to follow a religion

morals Ideas of right and wrong beliefs and behavior

New World The region that was explored and settled by Europeans from the 1500s onward. The term was applied to North, South, and Central America

outlaw To make illegal

remedy A medicine or cure for an illness

rival An enemy

seminary A religious school where young men were trained to become Catholic priests

Sulpicians An organization of Catholic priests dedicated to teaching students at seminaries

tamper To change something in secret

trek A difficult journey

tribe A group of people from the same family background who share customs, beliefs, and traditions

Index

1 2 3 4 5 6 7 8 9 0 Printed in the U.S.A. 4 3 2 1 0 9 8 7 6 5